Anonymous

Orderly book of General George Washington,

Commander in chief of the American armies, kept at Valley Forge, 18

May-11 June, 1778 - Vol. 1

Anonymous

Orderly book of General George Washington,
Commander in chief of the American armies, kept at Valley Forge, 18 May-11 June, 1778 - Vol. 1

ISBN/EAN: 9783337810979

Printed in Europe, USA, Canada, Australia, Japan

Cover: Foto ©ninafisch / pixelio.de

More available books at **www.hansebooks.com**

Orderly Book

of

General George Washington

*Commander in Chief of the
American Armies*

Kept at

Valley Forge, 18 May — 11 June, 1778

VT·CRESCIT

Lamson, Wolffe and Company

Boston, New York and London

MDCCCXCVIII

THE original of the Orderly Book here printed is preserved in the Boston Athenæum. The undersigned is indebted to the Trustees of that Institution for the privilege of publishing it. The orders are for the most part in the handwriting of Major Samuel Shaw. The War Department at Washington possesses several of Washington's Orderly Books, but none covering the period of the present volume.

APPLETON P. C. GRIFFIN.

BOSTON, February, 1897.

ORDERLY BOOK

———•o⊰⊷⊱o•———

Officers
for duty
Tomorrow
{
Brig. Gen¹. Patterson
Lt. Colº. Cropper
Major Conway
Brigade Major Marvin
Inspector from Learned's Brigade
}

The Commander in Chief has the pleasure to inform the Army, that the honorable Congress have been pleased to come to the following resolutions

IN CONGRESS, May 1 1778

Resolved Unanimously, That all Military officers commissioned by Congress who now are, or hereafter may be, in the Service of the United States, and shall continue to [serve?] during the war, and shall not hold an [office] of profit under these States or any office after the conclusion of the war, shall be [en]titled to receive for the term of seven y[ears] if they live so long, one half of the present pay of such Officers, — Provided, that no General Officers of the Cavalry, Artillery, or Infantry, shall be entitled to receive more than the one half of the pay of a colonel of such Corps respectively — and provided, that the resolution shall not extend to any officer in the service of the United States unless he shall have taken the oath of allegiance to and shall actually reside within some one of the United States.

Resolved unanimously that every non commissioned Officer and Soldier who hath enlisted or shall enlist into the service of these States for and during the war and shall continue therein to the end thereof, shall be entitled to receive the further reward of 80 dollars at the expiration of the war —

The whole Army are directed to prepare in the best manner possible for immediate and sudden movement

BRIGADE ORDERS

Officer of the Day Capt L^t McClure
Col^o Lamb gives the Orderly to Head Quarters & Col^o Crane to the Brigade —

DETAIL FOR GUARDS

	S	P	C	F	D	M	TOTAL
Crane	–	1	–	–	–	10	11
Lamb	1	1	1	1	1	13	18
Porter	–	–	1	–	–	16	17
	1	2	2	1	1	39	46

19th

Officers for duty Tomorrow
{ Brig Genl Wayne —
Col^o Greene — Lt Col^o Ballard
Brigade Major — Minnis
Inspector from Patterson's Brigade

Commanding Officers of Regiments are to make returns to the Q. M. General of the number of tents absolutely wanting in each, for such men as cannot be accommodated consistent with their health and comfort in huts. It will be relied upon in these returns, that none will make a larger demand than the real situation of their respective regiments requires. The Q. M. G. will make his issues upon these returns.

At a Genl. Court Martial whereof Col° Bauman was President the 13 Inst, John Reynolds Artificer in Major Pollard's Corps tried for striking Lieu^t. Hemmet found guilty and sentenced to receive one hundred lashes. The Commander in Chief approves the sentence and orders it executed on the grand parade tomorrow morning at guard mounting —

Samuel Raymond at the same Court tried for presenting a loaded musket at L^t. Hemmet. Upon due consideration the Court are of opinion that he is guilty of the charge exhibited against him; but the extreme and unpardonable warmth with which the officers conducted themselves, renders the action of the prisoners in some measure excusable, and operates with the Court so strongly in his favor that they only sentence him to be reprimanded by the commanding Officer of the company to which he belongs.

Also John Coffin tried for abusing Capt Gowerly when attempting to supress a riot on the other side of Schuylkill, found not guilty and acquitted —

The General approves the sentences and orders them to take place immediately —

The Sub and Brigade Inspectors, Majors of Brigade, and Adjutants of the Army will assemble at the Baron Stubens quarters at 10 o'clock precisely, where they will receive particular orders —

ADVERTISEMENTS. —

A stray Horse taken up in Gen¹ Scott's Brigade — Enquire of Cap⁴ Killpatrick —
Another in Gen¹. Poors Brigade, enquire of L⁴ Cherry
Also a number in Col Van Schaicks Reg⁴. at Cuckold's Town. —

BRIGADE ORDERS

Officer of the Day Cap⁴. Kingsbury —
Col⁰ Lamb gives the Orderly to Head Quarters & Col⁰ Procter to the Brigade —

DETAIL FOR GUARDS

	S	S	C	F	D	M	TOTAL
Crane	—	1	1	0	0	10	12
Lamb	—	1	—	—	—	13	14
Procter	1	—	1	1	1	16	20

20

Officers
for duty
Tomorrow
{ Brig. Gen¹. Maxwell
Col⁰ Chambers — Major Winslow
Brigade Major Claiborne
Inspector from Weedon's Brigade

BRIGADE ORDERS

Officer of the Day. Cap⁴ Eustis
Col⁰ Procter gives the Orderly to Head Quarters & Col⁰ Lamb to the Brigade

DETAIL FOR GUARDS

	S	S	C	F	D	M	TOTAL	
Crane	1	1	–	1	1	10	14	}46
Lamb		1	1	–	–	13	15	
Procter	–	–	1			16	17	
	1	2	2	1	1	39	46	

21ᵗ

Officers for duty Tomorrow
{ Brig. Genˡ Varnum
Lᵗ. Colᵒ Reed — Major Moore
Brigade Major McCormick
Inspector from Muhlenburgh

The Inspectors &ᶜ will attend at the Baron Stuben's quarters tomorrow at the hour appointed in the orders of the 19 instant.

If there are any persons in the Army who understand making thin Paper, such as bank notes are struck upon, they are desired to apply immediately to the Orderly Office, where they will be shewn a sample of the Paper — Officers commanding Regiments are to publish this in Regimental Orders —

Mʳ Vowles Adjutant in the Virgᵃ Regᵗ. is approved to do the duty of Brigade Major in Genˡ. Woodford's Brigade till further orders.

At a General Court Martial the 15 inst whereof Colᵒ Bowman was President, Capᵗ Cleaveland, of Colᵒ Michˡ. Jackson's Regiment, tried for behaving in an unofficerlike manner in refusing to do a tour of duty when duly notified, found not guilty of the charge exhibited against him, and acquitted with honor.

Although Capᵗ Cleaveland ought not to have been

warned for duty when return'd sick, yet the General cannot applaud the spirit which actuated him in refusing obedience to a positive order, and declining a tour of duty such a kind as might have been in all appearance easily performed by Cap'. Cleaveland in his circumstances — Cap'. Cleaveland is released from his arrest —

At a Brigade Court Martial whereof L'. Col°. Cropper was President, Cap'. Eward [*sic*] Hull of the 15 Virg'. Reg' tried for gaming when he ought to have been on the parade the 12 instant, unanimously found guilty of that part of the charge exhibited against him relative to gaming, but acquitted of nonattendance on the parade, and sentenced to be reprimanded by the Commanding Officer of the Brigade in present [*sic*] of all the officers thereof.

At the same Court Lieu'. Thomas Lewis of the same Reg'. tried upon a similar charge found guilty and sentenced the same as Cap' Hull.

The Commander in Chief, however unwilling to dissent from the judgement of a Court Martial, is obliged utterly to disapprove these sentences; the punishment being in his opinion entirely inadequate to the offence. A practice so pernicious in itself, as that of gaming, so prejudicial to good order and military discipline, so contrary to positive and repeated general orders, carried to so enormous a height as it appears, and aggravated certainly in the case of L'. Lewis, by an additional offence of no triffling military consequence — absence from parade, demanded a much severer penalty than simply a reprimand. — Cap' Hull and Lieu'. Lewis are to be released from arrest —

BRIGADE ORDERS

Officer of the Day Cap⁺ Lᵗ. Finley
Colᵒ Procter gives the Orderly to Head Quarters
& Colᵒ Crane to the Brigade —

DETAIL FOR GUARD

	S	S	C	F	D	M	TOTAL
Crane	–	I				10	11
Lamb	I	I	I	I	I	13	18
Procter	–	I	–	–	–	16	17
	I	2	2	I	I	39	46

22ᵈ

Officers
for duty
Tomorrow
{
Brig Genˡ Scott
Colᵒ Brewer — Major Hopkins
Brigade Major Berrien
Inspector from Late Conway's
}

The Auditors Office is removed to Jaˢ Cloyd's
within a mile and a half of the Pay Master Generals.

At a General Court Martial the 16 insᵗ. of which
Colᵒ Bowman is President Lieuᵗ. Edison of the Ger-
man Battalion tried for behaving in a manner unbecoming a gentleman and an officer in abusing
Colᵒ Nixon's family, unanimously found guilty of the
charge exhibited against him being a breach 21
Art. 14 Sec. Articles of War and sentenced to be
discharged from the service. — The Commander in
Chief approves the sentence and orders it to take
place immediately.

At a Brigade Court Martial the 18ⁱⁿˢᵗ· Major
Wallis President, Lᵗ Marks of the 11ᵗʰ Virgᵃ.

Reg^t. tried for not attending the parade on the 13 ins^t. and unanimously acquitted of the charge with honor.

Likewise, L^t. W^m. Powell tried upon the same charge and acquitted in like manner —

The General observes that sickness or indisposition is certainly a sufficient excuse for not attending the parade but it ought to be an established rule to signify it either personally or in writing thro' the Adj^t. to the Commanding Officer of the Regiment to which the Officer concerned shall belong. These Gentlemen in not doing this were dificient in the line of regularity and propriety. Hereafter the excuse shall not be admitted unless this rul · be observed except where any particular circumstances render the observance impracticable, which can rarely happen —

BRIGADE ORDERS

Officer of the Day Capt Porter
Col^o Lamb gives the Orderly to Head Q^{rs}.
& Col^o Crane to the Brigade.

DETAIL

	S	S	C	F	D	M	TOTAL
Crane			1			10	11
Lamb		1	-	-	-	13	14
Procter	1	1	1	1	1	16	21
	1	2	2	1	1	39	46

23

Officers for Duty Tomorrow
{
Brig Genl Patterson
Col^o Dayton M
Briggade Major Stagg
Inspector from Hunting^{tons} Brigade
}

Till some further arraignment [*sic*] of the Army is made Major Gen¹ Lee is to take Charge of the Division lately Commanded by Major Gen¹ Greene, and in Case of Action or any general Move of the Army, the three eldest Major Gen¹ˢ present fit for Duty are to Command the two Wings & 2ᵈ Line according to their Seniority —

The Commanding officers & Regᵗˢ & Corps will immediately apply upon the Coming of military Stores for all the arms and Accoutrements wanting for their Men —

The Q M of Brigades will also make out Returns, & apply for orders for ammunition to compleat each man with 40 rounds & two Flints — All officers are calld upon to see that their Men's Arms & Accoutrements are put in the best order possible, they will likewise take particular Care that their men have wooden Drivers fixed in their peices at the Hours of Exercise to prevent an unnecessary wait of Flints, they are not to be absent from Camp on any pretence whatsoever but be in actual Rediness to march at a Moments Warning —

Brigade Orders

Capᵗ Lieuᵗ Jones Officer of the Day —
Colᵒ Crane gives the Orderly to Head Qʳˢ
& Colᵒ Lamb to the Brigade —

Detail

	S	S	C	F	D	M	TOTAL
Crane	1	1	1	1	1	14	19
Lamb	–	–	1	–	–	11	12
Procter	–	1	–	–		14	15
	1	2	2	1	1	39	46

24th 1778

Officers for Duty to Morrow

Brigadier Wayne Co^l Patten, Major Sumner B: M: Bannister Inspector from Varnums Brigade

The Genl. Court Martial Whereof Co^l. Bowman is President is Disolved, another is Ordered to sit to Morrow Morning 9 O. Clock to try all Such persons as Shall be brought before them Co^l. Chambers will preside Each Brigade gives a Capt. for the Court. All persons Concerned to Attend — At a Brigade Court Martial May 22^d. 1778 — Lieu^t. Col Cropper president. Lieu^t Davis of the 11th. Virg^a. Reg^t. tried for Encouraging a soldier to stay away from his Reg^t. for Refusing when the soldier was Sent for by a Guard to let him go, to his Reg^t. and for Speaking Disrespectfully of the officer who sent the Guard who Sent the Guard [*sic*] a second time, upon Mature Deliberation the Court are of opinion he is not Guilty of Speaking Disrespectfully of the Officer who sent the Guard for Serj^t. Davis, tho' of Oppinion that his Detaining the Serj^t. was unwarrantable. But Considering that his Error Seemes to have Arose from what he thought was Doing his Duty Do Acquit him —

Lieu^t. Davis is Ordered to be Released from his Arrest —

BRIGADE ORDERS

Officer of the Day Capt Lt Brice

Col^o. Lamb gives the Orderly to Head Quarters & Col^o. Procter to the Brigade —

DETAIL

	S	S	C	F	D	M	TOTAL
Crane	–	1	1	–	–	14	16
Lamb	1	1	–	1	1	11	15
Procter	–	–	1	–	–	14	19
	1	2	2	1	1	39	46

25th

Officers for duty Tomorrow { Brig Gen¹ Muhlenburg
Col° Swift — Lᵗ Col° Hubley
Brigade Major Haskell
Inspector from MᶜIntosh's Brigᵉ.

The Regimental Surgeons will apply to the Flying Hospital store for hogs lard and sulpher — They are to make their returns more punctually on Mondays —

Several guns, packs & cartridge boxes belonging to some soldiers in the Army are left at the orderly office.

The Muster Mʳ. General and Commissary of Prisoners have removed their quarters to Mʳ. Evans' house half a mile north of Sullivan's bridge near Perkiomy Creek —

The Regᵗ. Pay Masters to give in their abstracts to the P. M. General immediately for examination for the Months of April.

At a Gen¹. Court Martial the 1st May — of which Col° Febiger was President, Lieuᵗ. Adams of the 10 Penᵃ Regᵗ. tried for " ungentlemanlike behavior in propagating a report that an officer of the 10 Penᵃ Regᵗ had behaved cowardly, in the action of

Germantown and, when desired by Col°. Hubley to
name the officer, for refusing to do it in an unbecoming manner" — unanimously found guilty of the
charge exhibited against him, being a breach of 21
Art. of the 14 Sect. Article of war, and sentenced
to be dismissed the service — His Excellency the
Commander in Chief approves the sentence, and
orders it to take place immediately.

AFTER ORDER

Signals will be given this afternoon in manœuvering by a small field piece. This notice is given
to prevent an alarm. —

BRIGADE ORDERS

Officer of the Day Capt. L^t. Cotnam
Col°. Procter gives the Orderly to Head Quarters —
& Col°. Crane to the Brigade

DETAIL

	S	S	C	F	D	M	TOTAL
Crane	–	–	1	–	–	14	15
Lamb	–	1	–		–	8	9
Procter	1	1	1	1	1	17	22
	1	2	2	1	1	39	46

Lieu^t. Ford is appointed to do duty as Adjutant
in Col°. Lamb's Reg^t. and is to be respected and
obeyed accordingly

26th

Officers
for duty
Tomorrow
{
Brig. Genl Poor
Col° Grayson, Lt Col° Wisenfeldt's
Brigade Major Learned
Inspector from Woodfords

The Commander in Chief perceiving that the Regimental returns materially differ in the number of sick absent from the Hospital reports, notwithstanding these were lodged with the Adjutant Generals that the regimental returns might be rectified and adjusted by them, calls upon the Commanding Officers of Regiments to make returns tomorrow to the Adjutant General specifying the names of all their sick absent, the places where they are and the times they were sent to them, that the difference above mentioned may be satisfactorily accounted for. In doing this the strictest regard to be paid to the Hospital reports.

An independent corps commanded by Capt. Selin are immediately to bury the offal & carrion near the black bull. The Com^g Genl of the Staff will in future apply to the commanding officer of that corps for a party to bury any offal which may be near his stall.

A Sub-Serj^t. Corp^l. & 8 men with the commissary from each brigade are to be put immediately into the vicinity of their respective Brigades to seize the liquors they may find in the unlicenced tipling houses. The Commissaries will give receipts for the liquors they shall seize and notify the inhabitants or persons living in the vicinity of camp that an unconditional seizure will be made of all liquors they shall presume to sell in future.

A Flag goes to Philadelphia tomorrow —

BRIGADE ORDERS

Officer of the day Capt Lieu^t. Powars —
Col^o Lamb gives the Orderly to Head Q^t.
& Col^o Crane to the Brigade —

DETAIL

	S	S	C	F	D	M	TOTAL
Crane	1	–	1	1	1	14	18
Lamb	–	1	–	–	–	8	9
Procter	–	1	1	–	–	17	19
	1	2	2	1	1	39	46

Officers for Duty tomorrow ⎰ Brig Gen Varnum
Col⁰ Read Mʳ Murray
B Major Ten Eyck
Inspector from Scott's Brigade

The Commanding Officers of Regᵗ are to make returns on Friday next of the Arms that were in posession of their respective Corps the 1ˢᵗ of Novʳ. last of those they have since delivered in, of those they have since drawn, & of those now in actual posession, tis expected they always have exact accounts kept of arms, Cloathing Camp Utensils &ᶜ furnished their men as they must be responsable for their due application. Major Genˡ. Mifflin having been permitted by Congress to repair to & serve in this Army is to take the Command of the Division late Lincolns. — The Field Officers of Regᵗˢ who have drawn Money from any of the public offices for recruiting their respective Corps are desired as soon as possible to furnish the Auditor of the Army with lists of Money advancd by them, their officers for that Service — Capt Turbedille is appointed aid de Camp to Major Genˡ Lee till further orders. & is to be respected accordingly — Officers are to see that the mud plastering around the Hutts be removd. & every other method taken to render them as airy as possible, they will also have the powder of a Musquet Cartridge burnt in each Hutt dayly to purify the Air, or a little Tar if it can be procur'd, the Commissary of military Stores will provide blank Cartridges for this purpose —

BRIGADE ORDER

Officer of the Day Capt. Cook
Col^o Crane gives the orderly to Head Q^s
& Col^o Lamb to the Brigade

DETAIL FOR GUARDS

	S	S	C	F	D	M	TOTAL
Crane		1	–	–	–	14	15
Lamb	1	–	1	1	1	8	12
Procter	–	1	1	–	–	17	19
	1	2	2	1	1	39	46

A Genl. Court Martial of which Lt Col^o Oswald is appointed President will set tomorrow at 9 o'clock at the Presidents quarters for the trial of such prisoners as shall be brought befor 'em.

Capt. Wilkenson
Capt. Eustis — Capt Van Heer — Capt Kingsbury
Capt. L^t. Browne — Capt. L^t. McClure.
2 Subs from Col^o Crane
2 from Col^o Lamb
2 from Col^o Procter
Members —
Capt L^t. Finley, Judge Advocate

28

Officers
for duty
Tomorrow
{ Brig. Gen¹ Scott
Col° Irvine — Lᵗ Col° Bassett
Brigade Major Johnson
Inspector from 1 Pennª Brigade

Commanding Officers of Brigades, in pursuance
of former orders to hold themselves in readiness to
march are to apply immediately to the Q M Gen¹ for
a sufficient number of waggons to transport their
baggage, and are to have their respective brigades
supplied as completely as possible with camp utensils, and necessaries of every kind requisite towards
taking the field. The Commissary will have a quantity of hard bread and salt meat prepared to issue
to the Army when called for; As we may expect
every moment to march the Army is to be prepared
in all respects for that purpose.

Guards of every kind are constantly to hold themselves in a collected state with their accoutrements
on, and ready to act at a moments warning. The
General forbids all exercise and diversions, particularly such as cause them to disperse and put off their
accoutrements, which is equally incomitant with the
safety and good discipline.

A Board of General Officers to set tomorrow
morning ten o'clock at Gen¹ Lee's quarters to
examine into Lᵗ Col° Regnier's claim of rank in
the N York line, and report their opinion thereon.
The other Lieuᵗ Colonels of that line present are
to attend. The Commander in Chief will lay before the Board the memorial presented by Lᵗ. Col°
Regnier with other papers.

A court of enquiry to set tomorrow to examine into the conduct of L⁺. Col°. Parks, reported to have been absent from camp without leave, and to have been negligent in his duty. All persons concerned will attend, Col° Johnson is appointed President; Col°. Parker, L⁺ Cols. Bunner and Starr, and Major Fenner will attend as Members at the Presidents quarters 9 oClock tomorrow morning. —

Returns from the several Brigades of such cloathing and necessaries as are absolutely wanting to be made next Saturday at orderly time.

28th

Brigade Orders

Cap⁺. L⁺. Bussey Officer of the Day
Col° Lamb gives the Orderly to Head Q⁺ˢ.
& Col° Procter to the Brigade.

Detail for Guards

	S	S	C	F	D	M	TOTAL
Crane	–	1	2	–	–	14	17
Lamb	–	1	–		–	8	9
Procter	1	–	–	1	1	17	20
	1	2	2	1	1	39	46

29

Officers for duty Tomorrow
{
Brig. Gen¹ Huntington
L⁺ Col° Burr — Major Still
Brigade Major Seely
Inspector from 2ᵈ Pennᵃ Brigade
}

The Commanding Officers of Regiments and Corps are not, under any pretence whatever (unless duty requires it) to permit their officers or men to

be absent from camp, that they may be ready to
march at an hours warning.

At a Gen¹. Court Martial, Col°. Chambers President the 25 instant, Cap⁺. Medaras, of the North
Carolina Brigade, tried for forgery — after mature
deliberation the Court are of opinion that Cap⁺ Ma-
daras is guilty of the charge exhibited against him
but as he could not have been actuated by motives
self interested or injurious to Cap⁺ Jones, the Gentleman whose name he signed, and as he had before
been perfectly acquainted with Cap⁺. Jones's senti-
ments, the Court (thinking his crime, tho' he is yet
truly blameworthy, alleviated by these circumstances)
do sentence him to be reprimanded in General
Orders.

The Commander in Chief approves the Sentence,
and is much concerned to find that an Officer in this
Army, should presume to sign a Brother Officer's
name without his permission. Cap⁺ Medaras is ordered to be released from his arrest.

At the same Court Wᵐ Whiteman Waggoner,
tried for desertion and sentenced to receive sixty
lashes — approved and ordered to be put in execution tomorrow morning on the grand parade at
grand mounting —

Also, John Cline of the 10th Penn³. Reg⁺. tried
for desertion and attempting to escape to the
enemy, and for stealing a horse — found guilty of
both charges and sentenced to receive 200 lashes,
100 for each crime. The Gen¹. approved the Sentence, and orders it put it execution this evening
at roll call at the head of the Regiment to which
he belongs

Also, John Wood Serj⁺. in the 8 Penn³. Reg⁺. tried for desertion and attempting to the enemy, acquited and ordered to be released from his confinement.

ADVERTISEMENT

On the night of the 27th inst. James Barry an Inhabitant was robbed of £160 Cont¹. Money, 13 hard dollars, a diamond ring, silver spoons, buckles gold buttons, a sword, and some valuable men's & women's wearing apparell, & many other articles. Fifty Dollars reward will be given to any person that will discover the robbers, that the Owner may recover his articles. All Officers are desired to order the strictest enquiry to be made that the Villains may be brought to justice, as it is supposed they belong to the Army

BRIGADE ORDERS

Officer of the Day — Cap⁺. Browne.
Col°. Procter gives the Orderly to Head Q⁺ˢ.
& Col Crane to the Brigade —

DETAIL FOR GUARDS

	S	S	C	F	D	M	TOTAL
Crane	–	1	–	–	–	14	15
Lamb	1	1	1	1	1	8	13
Procter		–	1	–	–	17	18
	1	2	2	1	1	39	46

The Quarter Mast⁺ˢ. of Reg⁺. is to make returns by Eight O Clock this evening, to the Brig⁺. Q⁺ M⁺ of the Marques Horsmans Tents Common Tents & Knap Sacks, Camp Kettles & Canteens, and

what Officers are posses'd of the Marques & Horse-
mans Tents, as no further Issues can be made till
such returns are compleated, — They will also pro-
duce at the same time if possible or as soon as it is
convenant returns Signed by them, for such Stores
& Camp equipage as have been Issued since the
22^d of March last, specifying what part thereof has
been Issued through the hands of Brig^d Q M^{rs}. in
order that the same may be duly compared with
the Genl Acco^t of Issues.

The General expects a punctual compliance with
the above order, and that the returns of cloathing
call'd for in yesterdays orders be made out in order
to be carried in by the Brigade Major at the pre-
cise time therein mentioned.

30th 1778

Officers for Duty to Morrow

Brigadier Patterson Co^l. Bradley — B: M: Marshall
Inspector from Poor's Brigade

The Commanding Officers of Brigades are to
Appoint a sufficient Number of Proper Officers
to be left in Charge of the Sick and such others
of their Respective Brigades as will be Enable to
march with them in Case the Army moves from
the present Camp —

The Regimental Surgeons will make out and
Lodge, with the surgeon Genl. of the flying Hospital Exact Returns, of the sick belonging to their
several Reg^{ts}. who shall be left in Camp when the
Army Marches — The board of Genl. officers held
agreeable to the Order of the 28th Ins^t have made

the following Report, the claims of Lieu^t. Col^o.
Regnier & the other Lieu^t. Col^s. of the State of
N. York — Respecting their standing in Rank,
being considered, the board are of Oppinion that
Lieu^t. Col. Regnier will take Rank of those Gentleman on Courts Martial Detachments on all Duties
from the Line, but that the[y] Command him in the
line of the State, for notwithstanding Lieu^t. Col.
Regnier Rank as Lieu^t. Col. was Anteceeded to
theirs in the Line yet his Appointment in that
state was postirior The Commander in Chief
Approves the above Report

At a Brigade Genl Court Martial May 27th 1778
Lieu^t Col. Cropper, president Capt. Hull of the 15th V :
Reg^t. tried 1^{stly} being so far Ellivated with Liquor
when on the parade for Exercising, on the 14th Ins^t.
as rendered him imCapable in doing his Duty with
precission. 2dly for accusing Lieu^t. Saml. Beans
Jones of not deposing the truth when Called on
Both to give Evidence against him on the 18th. Inst.
acquited of the 1st. Charge but found guilty of the 2^d
& Sentenced to be Reprimanded by the Command-
ing Officer of the Brigade in presence of all the
Officers therein — Capt. Hull is Ordered to be released from his Arrest. — At a Genl. Court Martial
May 28th 78, Col. Chambers President Ensign James
Walker of Col. Guests Reg^t. tried 1^{tly} Deserting a
Waggon he had in his Charge at the Appearance
of one of our Light Horse and loosing his party
in his flight. 2dly for telling several falshoods in
Relating the Events when Returning to Camp
Unanimously found guilty of the Charges Exhib-
ited against him, being breaches of 5th Article 18

Sec^t. of 21st Article 14th Section of the Articles of
War, and Sentenced to be Cashiered — The Com-
mander in Chief Approves the Sentence and Orders
it to take place Immediatly.

At the same Court John Lewis Drew Co^l. Angel's
Reg^t. tried for threatning to take the lives of Several
Officers of that Reg.^{t} found guilty & sentenced to
Receive 60 Lashes —

Approved & ordered to be put' in Execution at
Roll Call this evening at the Head of the Reg^t. he
belongs —

A Quantity of Continental Currency lately found
in the hands of Lieu^t. Dexter. Co^l. Angel's Reg^t. the
owner may Receive the same by proving his prop-
erty.

BRIGADE ORDERS.

Col^o. Cranes Regiment is to be mustered on
Monday next at ten oClock —

Col^o. Lamb's & Col^o. Procter's at the same hour on
Tuesday —

& Col^o Harrison's on Wednesday —

The Officers will be careful to have their Muster
Rolls made out correctly, and see that their men
have their blankets neatly rolled up, as they must
parade with them on. —

Capt. Brown's & Capt. Dorsey's Companies are
annexed to Col^o Harrison's Regiment with whom
they are to do duty till further orders —

Officer of the Day Capt. Seward
Col^o Procter gives the Orderly to Head Q^{rs}.
& Col^o Harrison to the Brigade.

DETAIL

	SUB	S	C	F & D	M	TOTAL
Crane	–	1	1	–	12	14
Lamb & Kingsbury	–	1		–	7	8
Procter	1	–		2	7	10
Harrison & 2 Companies	–	–	1	–	19	20
	1	2	2	2	45	52

31

Officers for duty Tomorrow ⎰ Brig Gen¹ Wayne
L͐. Col° Livingston L͐ Colº Miller
Brigade Major Marvin
Inspector from Glover's Brigade

The 2ᵈ State Regᵗ of Virginia is for the present
to be annexed to Muhlenburg's Brigade, and Colº
Van Schaicks regiment till further orders is in like
manner to be joined to the 2ᵈ Pennᵃ Brigade in lieu
of the 8 Penᵃ Regᵗ. which is to be detached on other
service.

A Surgeon from each Brigade is to remain in
camp to attend the sick of it which shall be left
behind under the direction of Doctʳ. Hutchinson, till
relieved by surgeons from the general hospital, then
they are immediately to join their respective regiments —

Men in the small pox, or under enoculation, are
to be comprehended in the number of the sick —
Regimental Medicine Chests are to go on with the

Army — A Sufficient number of Camp Kettles must be left for the use of the sick.

Commanding Officers of Regiments will assist the Regimental surgeons in procuring as many women of the army as can be prevailed on to serve as nurses to them, for which they will be paid the usual price. Orderlies are also to be left; one to every 20 sick men, who are to be such as, for want of cloathing, from lameness and the like, are least fit to march with the Army, but at the same time, capable of this duty. — A Commissary is likewise to be left to supply the sick with provisions. A commissioned officer to every fifty men is to remain, and a Field Officer to superintend the whole. The arms of the sick in each regiment are to supply as far as may be necessary the deficiency of those unfit for duty. If any remain they are to be left in care of the officer who stays with the sick — The Vaults are to be well covered before the Brigades quit the ground.

Commanding Officers of Divisions and all others are to pay the strictest attention that no women be suffered on any pretence to get into the waggons of the Army on the march.

Some Hospital Tent poles were delivered at the Q M Gen^{ls} store through mistake. Those who have them in possession are desired to return them immediately —

Brigade Orders

Officer of the Day Capt. Lee
Col°. Harrison gives the Orderly to Head Q^{rs}.
& Col° Crane to the Brigade

DETAIL FOR GUARDS

	SUB	S	C	F & D	M	TOTAL
Crane	–	–	I	–	10	11
Lamb	–	I	–	–	6	7
Procter	–	I	I	–	9	11
Harrison	I	–	–	2	20	23
	I	2	2	2	45	52

At a Brigade Court Martial whereof Lt Col^o. Oswald was President, the 28, 29, & 30, Instant, Serj^t. John Nevil of Col^o Lamb's Reg^t. tried for " losing a bullock by neglect when Serj^t. of the Commissary's guard" was by them unanimously acquitted.

Jon^a Gill of Capt. Browns Company, tried for " drunkeness on his post " pleaded guilty, and was sentenced to receive 50 lashes.

Ja^s Whaling, Drummer of Col^o Procter's Reg^t. tried for " desertion and attempting to get into Philadelphia " plead guilty. The court in consideration of his youth, and his having received no pay or bounty except some cloathes, as appeared from Col^o Procters evidence, do Sentence him to receive only 30 lashes.

Michael Nash, of Capt. Kingsbury's Company, tried for " drunkeness on duty, and absenting himself from his guard " plead guilty, and sentenced to receive 50 lashes —

John Gibbons, of Col^o. Procter's Reg^t. tried for " absenting himself from camp without leave " was sentenced to receive 50 lashes —

The General approves the sentence & orders Serj^t Nevil to be released from his confinement —

Some circumstances appearing in favor of Ja⁵ Whaling, the 30 lashes are remitted — The punishment order'd the others is to be inflicted tomorrow morning at guard mounting at the head of the regiments to which they respectively belong.

The Court Martial whereof Lᵗ. Colᵒ Oswald is President is dissolved.

JUNE I

Officers for duty Tomorrow
{ Brig. Genˡ. Muhlenburg
Colᵒ Wigglesworth — Major Church
Brigade Major Minnis
Inspector from Learneds Brigade

Colᵒ Cortlandt is appointed to tarry in camp to superintend the sick left on the ground when the Army moves, and to send on the recovered men properly officered to join their respective Corps and Major   will repair to the Yellow Springs and the hospitals near Camp, and superintend the Sick there. They will apply tomorrow at the Orderly office for written instructions —

The following will be observed as a standing model for the order of march, whether of the whole Army, a Division, Brigade, or Battalion. It may happen that some changes may be necessary in the strength and number of the advanced, rear, and flank guards, and in their relative distances to each other and to the main body, &ᶜᵃ.; which are to be determined according to particular circumstances, and which the officers commanding will judge of. — But the general principles and rules here laid down are, in all cases, to be practised, only with such variations in applying them as different situations may require.

When a Battalion receive orders to march, each company forms before its own quarters; the Captain having inspected into their arms and accoutrements conducts it to the regimental parade, where the Field Officers inspect the whole, forms each Battalion into 8 plattoons for charging, agreeable to instructions given, and march it by plattoons to the rendezvous. When only one battalion marches, the Colonel orders out an advanced and rear Guard, each consisting of 1 Lieu'. 3 Non-Com-Officers 1 Drum and 20 privates — A Brigade composed of several Battalions has an advanced and rear guard, each consisting of 1 Captain, 2 Subs, 6 N. C. O. & 40 or 50 privates. — When several Brigades march together each Brigade furnishes a proportionable number for the advanced and rear guards — When the whole Army marches the new guards of the day form the advanced guard, and the old ones the rear guard. The new guards being assembled on the grand parade the Brigadier of the day forms them into a Battalion of 8 plattoons, the eldest field officer of the day takes the command of it, and marches at the head of the column. The Brigadier of the preceeding day having assembled the old guards, forms them in the same manner, the eldest Field Officer taking the com-mand and marching in the rear of the column — The advanced guard should be from 50 to 200 paces in front of the column. Each advanced guard should send forward a detatchment to serve as an advanced guard to itself; and that detatchment should also send out a patrole in front, each an hundred paces in front of the other — Thus, 1 Capt 2 Subs, 6 n. c. off. — 1 Drum, & 50 men will send out a non c. off. & 12 men — and that N. C. O. will also advance 4 men in his front. An advanced guard of a Lieu^t. & 20 men will advance 1 n. c. o. & 8 men, who will also advance 2 men in his front. The rear guard will observe the same rules, sending its detatchments in the rear as the advanced guard does in front —

When a Brigade, Division, or the Army, marches by the right it is supposed the enemy is on the left — and the contrary. — Each Battalion will therefore send out on the flank exposed to the enemy, 1 Sub, 2 N. C. O. & 16 men as a flank guard, who will march in a plattoon by files from the right opposite the centre of the battalion, at the distance of 80 or 100 paces from the column.

When the Army marches in 2 columns, the right column has its flank guard on its right and the left column on its left, — when in one column, and the position of the enemy uncertain, guards must be sent out on both flanks. The advanced, rear, and flank guards must always have their bayonets fixed. Whenever the grounds will permit, the battalions must march by plattoons; during the march each Colonel must stay before his battalion, and each Captain & Subaltern before his plattoon; the intervals between the battalions and plattoons must be strictly observed during the march — When there is a creek or defile to pass, the Brigadiers must stop till their Brigade have passed, and the Colonels till their respective battalions have passed. They will take care that the men pass with as large a front, and as quick, as possible. The advanced guard having passed the defile should take such a situation as to be able to see all around, and shall send out patroles 500 paces round. The head of the column halts before it enters the defile to let the plattoons get at half distance, and when half the column has got through it halts till the whole has passed and then continues its march. When the road will not permit to march by plattoons, the march is to be made by 4 in front, in the following manner,—each officer divides his plattoon into sections—for example, a plattoon of 16 files makes 4 sections; they will break off by the right or left, each section 2 paces from the other, and continue the march — If a plattoon has 15 files the last section will have 3 files — if 14, the last will have 4 men in one rank, if 13 files the last will have 5 files — When marching in this order by the right the officers commanding plattoons will be on the left of the first section, the Serj' on the right stays in his place, and the Officers & N. C. O. who were in the rear will be on the right flank. If they march in this order by the left the C. Off. of the plattoon remains on the right of the first section and the others on the left flank; so that by wheeling the sections the plattoon will be formed, and each officer and n. c. o. will be in his place.

During the march each Officer must keep his plattoon in order; the Officers & N. C. O. in the rear must prevent the soldiers leaving their ranks on any account. If the soldiers have occasion for water the officer must send a n. c. o. with some men to fill their canteens and the n. c. o. must bring them back to their plattoons immediately.

The flank guard will never suffer any non c. officer or soldier to pass them during the march, and the rear guard will take care to bring up all stragglers.

BRIGADE ORDERS.

Officer of the Day Capt Sargent
Col^o Harrison gives the Orderly to Head Quarters
— & Col^o Crane to the Brigade

DETAIL FOR GUARDS

	S	S	C	F & D	M	TOTAL
Crane	I	I	I	2	10	15
Lamb	—	—	o	—	6	6
Procter	—	—	—	—	9	9
Harrison	—	I	I	—	20	22
	I	2	2	2	45	52

A Brigade Court Martial to sit tomorrow morning 9 oclock, at a tent near the General's house — for the trial of such prisoners as shall be brought before them —

Lt Col^o Du Plissis is appointed President

Capt Cook ⎫
Capt Lt Powers ⎪
     Cotnam ⎬ Members ⎰ 2 Subs from Col^o Crane
     Coltman ⎪   { 1 D^o — Lamb
2 Capt L^{ts} from ⎪   ⎱ 1 D^o — Procter
Col^o Harrison's Reg^t. ⎭   2 D^o — Harrison
    Capt. L^t. Duffey Judge Adv^v.

BRIGADE AFTER ORDERS

The Order for a General Court martial, of which L^t. Col^o Du Plissis was appointed President this day, is countermanded —

2^d

Officers
for duty
Tomorrow
{
Brig. Genl. Poor
Col^o. Bowman.   Lt Col^o Beauford
Brigade Major Claiborne
Inspector from Patterson's Brigade
}

At a General Court Martial of which Col° Chambers was President, May the 29, L^t. Col° Grey, of the 12th Penn^a Regiment tried for " ungentlemanlike behavior in entering into private contracts with the soldiers of his Regt for the deficiency of rations, by which means and other unwarrantable practices, the soldiers are defrauded of a considerable sum of money — found guilty of the charge exhibited against him, being a breach of the 21st Art. 14 Sect. Articles of War, and sentenced to be cashiered, and that (agreeable to the 22 Art. 14 Sec.) his name, place of abode, crime and punishment be published in the News Papers in and about camp and of that particular State from which he came, or in which he usually resides.   His Excellency the Commander in Chief approves the sentence and orders it to take place.

At the same Court, L^t. Webb of the 7th Virg^a Reg^t was tried for " disobedience of orders, for going on duty in a hunting shirt, after confessing he had a coat and being desired that if he had no regard to his own appearance to have some for the credit of his regiment, and therefore not to appear in so unofficerlike a manner " — found guilty and sentenced to be reprimanded by the Officer commanding the regiment to which he belongs, in presence of the Officers of the Reg^t. — The General approves the sentence and orders it put in execution tomorrow morning at roll call —

BRIGADE ORDERS

Officer of the Day — A Captain from Col° Harrison's Reg'.
Col° Lamb gives the Orderly to Head Q'ʳˢ
& Col° Procter to the Brigade —

DETAIL

	S	S	C	F & D	M	TOTAL
Crane	–	–	–	–	10	10
Lamb	1	1	1	2	6	11
Procter	–	–	–	–	9	9
Harrison	–	1	1	–	20	22
	1	2	2	2	45	52

3ᵈ

Officers for duty Tomorrow
{ Brig-Gen¹ — Varnum
L' Col° Regnier — Maj'. Porter
Brigade Major M°Cormick
Inspector from Weedon's Brigade

Thomas Shanks, on full conviction of his being a spy in the service of the Enemy before a board of General Officers held yesterday by order of the Commander in Chief, is adjudged worthy of death — he is therefore to be hanged tomorrow morning at guard mounting, at some convenient place near the grand parade.

At a Gen¹. Court Martial the 1ˢᵗ instant, Col° Chambers President, Lieut Toomy of Col° Gist's Reg'. detached to the 3ᵈ Maryland Regiment tried for disobedience of orders, found guilty and sentenced to be reprimanded by the Commanding Officer of the Brigade in presence of the Officers of the Brigade to which he belongs. The Commander in Chief approves the Sentence and orders it to take place tomorrow morning at roll call —

BRIGADE ORDERS

Officer of the Day — Capt Lt Duffee —
Col^o Harrison gives the Orderly to Head Q^{rs}.
& Col^o Crane to the Brigade —

DETAIL FOR GUARDS

	S	S	C	F & D	M	TOTAL
Crane	0	0	I	—	10	11
Lamb	0	I	—	—	4	5
Procter	I	I	—	2	11	15
Harrison	—	—	I	—	20	21
	I	2	2	2	45	52

When Commissions shall be issued to fill the vacancies in the Corps of Artillery they will be dated at the time the vacancies happened, according to the usual method —

Officers commanding Pieces are to be very careful that no waggoners are, *on any pretence whatever*, suffered to lodge in their waggons. Any one found sleeping in a waggon will be punished and the officer to whom such waggon shall belong called to a severe account.

4th

Officers for duty Tomorrow
- Brig. Genl. Scott.
- Lt Col^o North — Major Hawes
- Brigade Major Berrien
- Inspector from Muhlenburg.

The following Resolve of Congress, the operation
of which has been heretofore prevented by the particular circumstances of the Army, is in future to be
punctually observed.

IN CONGRESS, Nov. 19th 1776.

Resolved That on any sick or disabled non commissioned officer or soldier being sent to any hospital or sick quarters, the Captain or Commandant of
the troop or company to which he belongs shall
send to the Surgeon or Director of the said Hospital, or give to the N. C. O. or soldier so in the hospital or quarters a certificate countersigned by the
Pay Master of the Regiment (if he be with the reg^t.)
of what pay is due to such N. C. O. or private at the
time of his entering the hospital or quarters, and
the Capt. or Com^t. of the Troop or Company shall
not receive the pay of the said soldier in Hospital
or quarters or include him in any pay abstract during his continuance therein. And in case any N. C.
O. or soldier shall be discharged from the hospital
or quarters as unfit for further service, a certificate
shall be given him by the Surgeon or Director of
what pay is then due to him, and the said N. C. O.
or Soldier so discharged shall be entitled to receive
his pay at any pay office or from any pay master in
the service of the United States, the said Pay Master keeping such original certificate to prevent im-
positions and giving the N. C. O. or soldier his
discharge or a certified copy thereof, mentioning at
the same time his having been paid. — That this
Resolution be transmitted to the Commanders in
Chief in the several departments to be by them

given out in orders and then delivered to the directors of the hospitals in each department who are to cause the same to be fixed up in some conspicuous place or places in every military Hospital for the information of all concerned.

Commanding Officers of Regiments are immediately to make returns to the Com^y of Military Stores of the Arms actually wanting in their respective Corps to complete the number of men fit for duty in each. Agreeable to which the Com^y is forthwith to issue the arms now in store.

All Persons whatever are forbid selling liquor to the Indians. If any sutler or soldier shall presume to act contrary to this prohibition, the former will be dismissed from camp, and the latter receive severe corporal punishment.

On the march L^t. Col^o. Fleury will be attached to General Lee's Division — Lt Col^o Daviss to Genl. Lord Stirlings — Lt Col^o Barber to Genl. Mifflins — M^r. Ternant to Genl Marquis De La Faÿettee's — Lt Col^o Brooks to Genl. Baron De Kalb's —, and as they will not be employed on the march in exercising or manœuvering the troops they are to fill the office of Adjutant General, each in his respective Division —

BRIGADE ORDERS

Officer of the Day — A Captain Lieutenant from Col^o Harrison's Reg^t.
Col^o Crane gives the Orderly to Head Q^{rs}.
& Col^o Harrison to the Brigade —

DETAIL

	S	S	C	F & D	M	TOTAL
Crane	–	I	I	–	10	12
Lamb	–	–	–	–	4	4
Procter	–	–	I	–	11	12
Harrison	I	I	–	2	20	24
	I	2	2	2	45	52

Regimental Courts Martial are to sit tomorrow for the trial of Prisoners now in confinement belonging to their respective Regiments —

5th

Officers
for duty
Tomorrow

⎰ Brig. Gen¹ Huntington
⎱ L¹ Colᵒ Vose — Major Peters
⎰ Brigade Major Stagg
⎱ Inspector from late Conway's.

A Court of Enquiry, whereof Colᵒ Wigglesworth is appointed President, will sit tomorrow morning at 10 °clock at the President's quarters, at the request of L¹. Colᵒ Du Plissis, to enquire into his conduct on the different occasions mentioned in a letter from the Commander in Chief to Congress in his behalf, and into the truths of the facts on which the representation contained in it were founded, and of the several matters urged by the Officers of Artillery to the contrary, in a letter from them to the Commander Chief. All persons concerned will attend — L¹ Colᵒ Dearborn & Butler — Majors Hay & Campbell — Members.

Cap¹ Lawrence Keene of the Regiment late Patten's is appointed Aid de Camp to Major General Mifflin, and is to be obeyed as such.

A Captain from Weedon's Brigade & a Sub from the 1 Penn^a. are to repair immediately to the Hospitals at the yellow springs to relieve Capt Wallace and Lieu^t. Sweringen. They will call at the Orderly Office for Instructions.

At a General Court Martial whereof Col° Chambers was President, the 27 ulto L^t. McDonald of the 3^d Penn^a. Reg^t tried for "unofficer and ungentlemanlike behavior in taking 2 mares and a barrel of carpenter's tools on the lines, which mares he conveyed away, and sold the tools at private sale — and with insulting behavior in refusing to comply with his arrest." After mature deliberation, the Court, taking into consideration several circumstances are unanimously of opinion that altho L^t. McDonald is guilty of the facts alledged in the first charge that they do not amount to unofficer or ungentlemanlike behavior, and do acquit him of it, and likewise of the second. —

The Commander in Chief is far from being satisfied of the propriety of L^t. Mc Donald's conduct — he knows of no authority under which he had a right to seize the horses in question and to apply them in the manner he did — he approves still less of the measures taken with respect to the tools. If the probability of their being carried into the enemy arises by a disaffected person justified the seizure, nothing can justify the applying them, as appears to have been intended, to private emolument; to the injury of the right owner, who was an absent and innocent person, who had only lodged them in the care of the other during his absence. They ought immediately to have been reported to and deposited with the Q^r M General. — L^t. McDonald is released from arrest. —

Genl Poor's, Varnums, Huntington's 1st & 2 Penn^a and late Conway's Brigades and the Artillery to receive their pay for the months of Feby and March this day — Woodford's, Scott's and the North Carolina Brigades tomorrow — Glover's Pattersons and Learneds the 7th instant, Weedon's Muhlen-burg's the first & 2^d Maryland, the 8th.

Brigade Orders

A Genl. Court Martial in the Corps of Artillery of which Col^o Harrison is hereby appointed President, will sit tomorrow morning at 9 o'clock at the President's Tent for the trial of such persons as shall be brought before them —

Capt. Rice — Capt. Wells — 1 Capt. 1 Capt. Lieu^t. & 2 Lieutenants from Col^o Harrison's Reg^t. — Capt. Lt Dane — 2 Lieuts from Col^o Cranes Reg^t. — 1 from Col^o Lamb's and 2 from Col^o Procters Reg^t. will attend as members.

Capt L^t. Powars — Judge Advocate.

Officer of the Day — Capt L^t. Coltman.
Orderly to H^d Q^{rs}. — Harrison
to ye Brigade Crane.

Detail for Guards

	S	S	C	F&D	M	TOTAL
Crane	–	–	1	–	10	11
Lamb	–	1	–	–	4	5
Procter	–	1	–	–	11	12
Harrison	1	0	1	2	20	24
	1	2	2	2	45	52

6th

Officers for duty Tomorrow { Brig Genl. Patterson
Lt Colo Coleman — Major Moore
Brigade Major Bannister
Inspector from Huntington's

At a General Court Martial whereof Colo Chambers was President the 2 Inst Capt. Stake of the 10 Penna. Regiment tried for "propagating a report that Colo George Nagle was seen on the 15 of May drinking either tea or coffee in Sergt. Howeraft's tent, with his whore, her mother, the said Howeraft and his family to the prejudice of good order and military discipline." The Court having considered the charge and evidence are unanimously of opinion that Capt. Stake's justification is sufficient, and do acquit him of the charge exhibited against him — The General approves the acquital.

At the same Court Lt. Saml. Jones of the 15 Virga. Regt. tried for "concealing, and denying that he had in his possession, a pair of mittens belonging to Capt Hull — 2dly for gaming on the 12 of May and at sundry other times. 3dly for behaving in a manner unbecoming an Officer and Gentleman in treating Capt Hull with abusive language while under an arrest, and endeavoring to incense the Officers of his Regiment against him." The Court having considered the charge and evidence are of opinion that Lieut. Jones is guilty of the charges exhibited against him, and do sentence him to be discharged the service.

The General is entirely disposed to believe from

the representations he has received in favor of Lieu^t.
Jones, that he was incapable of having retained the
gloves with a fraudulent intention; but as he has
been clearly proved to have been guilty of the pernicious practice of *gaming*, which will invariably
meet with every mark of his disapprobation, he confirms the sentence of dismissing Lieu^t Jones.

At the same Court Lieu^t. John Roberts, of the 2^d
North Carolina Regiment tried, — 1st for behaving
in a scandalous, infamous manner — 2dly for absenting himself from camp without leave." The Court
having considered the charges and evidence are
unanimously of opinion that L^t. John Roberts is not
guilty of the charges exhibited against him, and do
acquit him —

The General approves the acquital — but is sorry
to see little personal bickerings between officers,
which cannot with propriety be drawn into military
offences, made the subjects of a court martial —

BRIGADE ORDERS

Officer of the Day.   Capt. L^t. Bursey
Col^o Harrison gives the Orderly to Head Q^{rs}.
& Col^o Crane to the Brigade

DETAIL FOR GUARDS

	S	S	C	F&D	M	— TOTAL
Crane	1	—	—	2	10	13
Lamb	—	1	—	—	4	5
Procter	—	—	1	—	11	12
Harrison	—	1	1	—	20	22
	1	2	2	2	45	52

At a Brigade Court Martial held this day, whereof Col° Harrison is President, George Deloney
of Col°. Crane's Regiment tried for " desertion " —
pleaded guilty, and was sentenced to receive one
hun'd lashes — also, John Gill of Col° Harrison's
Regt. tried for being drunk on his post — pleaded
guilty and was sentenced to receive fifty lashes —
But many circumstances appearing in favor of the
Prisoner, the Court recommend him for mercy. —

The General approves the above sentences, remits
the punishment ordered Gill — and forgives Delony
also, in whose favor some particular circumstances
have appeared.

7th

Officers for duty Tomorrow
{
Brig Gen¹ Wayne
L¹ Col° Haskill — Major Mentges
Brigade Major Haskill
Inspector from Varnum's.
}

The General Court Martial whereof Col° Chambers is President is dissolved and another ordered to
sit at the usual place to morrow for the trial of all
such prisoners as shall be brought before them —
Col° Livingston will preside — Each Brigade gives
a Captain for the Court.

A General Court Martial to sit tomorrow at 9
°Clock at the gulf mill to try all such persons as
shall be brought before them. L¹. Col° Smith will
preside — 4 Captains and 8 Subalterns from Col°.
Jackson's detatchment will attend as members.

The Court of Enquiry whereof Col° Johnson was
President the 29th ult°. report as follows. The Court
duly considering the charge exhibited against L¹

Col° Park, and his defence, are of opinion that he is guilty of having been absent from camp without leave but that he is not guilty of negligence of duty while in camp. The Court taking into considera- tion the peculiar circumstances attending Lᵗ Col° Parks absence, and the punishment he has already endured in consequence of his arrest and suspen- sion from duty, beg leave to recommend him to his Excellency as worthy of acquital. — The General restores Lᵗ. Col° Park to his command.

The Hon'ble the Congress have been pleased to come to the following Resolutions respecting the establishment of the Army.

" In Congress, May 27 1778
&ᶜ. as per printed Copy annexed.

(Inserted between pages 66 & 67 of the original is
a printed Act of Congress
dated 27ᵗʰ May 1778,
Entitled
The Establishment of the
American Army.)

All officers will be careful to make themselves well acquainted with the Establishment, and govern themselves accordingly.

The Commissaries will be particularly observant of what relates to their department with respect to rations and subsistence money.

Till the Regiments shall be arranged agreeable to this establishment the nomination of regimental staff officers according to the mode here pointed out is to be suspended.

BRIGADE ORDERS

Officer of the Day   Capt Burwell
Col^o Crane gives the Orderly to Head Q^{rs}.
Col^o Procter to the Brigade. —

DETAIL FOR GUARDS.

	S	S	C	F&D	M	TOTAL
Crane	—	0	1	—	10	11
Lamb	1	1	—	2	4	8
Procter	—	—	—	—	11	11
Harrison	—	1	1	—	20	22
	1	2	2	2	45	52

8th.

Officers
for duty
Tomorrow

{
Brig. Genl. Muhlenburg
Lt Col^o Ramsey — Major Talbot
Brigade Major Alden
Inspector from N^o Carolina Brigade.
}

Capt. John Mercer of the 3^d Virg^a. Reg^t is appointed to act as Aid de Camp to Major General Lee, and is to be accordingly respected —

BRIGADE ORDERS

Officer of the Day.   Capt Lt Meredith
Col^o Harrison gives the Orderly to Head Q^{rs}.
& Col^o Crane to the Brigade

DETAIL FOR GUARDS.

	S	S	C	F&D	M	TOTAL
Crane	—	—	—	—	10	10
Lamb	—	—	—	—	4	4
Procter	1	1	1	2	11	16
Harrison	—	1	1	—	20	22
	1	2	2	2	45	52

9th

Officers
for duty
Tomorrow

{ Brig. Genl. Woodford
  Col°. Smith & Major Pauling
  Brigade Major Johnson
  Inspector from Woodfords Brig —

After the dismission of the old guards the Brigadier and field officers of the preceeding day are to assemble at the provost guard and examine into the charges against the several prisoners there, and the circumstances attending them and to discharge all such as shall appear to be improperly confined, or the length of whose imprisonment may be deemed a sufficient punishment for their crimes, or whose offences are so triffling as to make the process of a General Court Martial unnecessary. — This to be a standing Order. — They are also to send to their Brigade and Regiments all those who are to be tried by Brigade or Regimental Courts. —

Three Captains and 9 Lieutenants are wanted to officer the Company of Sappers. As this Corps will be a school of Engineering, it opens a prospect to such Gentlemen as enter it and will pursue the necessary studies with diligence, of becoming Engineers and rising to the important employments attatched to that profession, such as the direction of fortified places &^c. The qualifications required of the Candidates are that they be *natives* and have a knowledge of the mathematicks and drawing, or at least be disposed to apply themselves to those studies — They will give in their names at Head Quarters —

The Army is to take a new camp tomorrow morning at 8 o'Clock. The whole is to be in readiness accordingly, and to march to the respective grounds of encampment, which will be pointed out for each Division by the Q. M^r. General.

At a Division Court Martial the 7th instant, L^t. Col^o Badlam President, Adj^t Allen of Col^o Mich^l. Jacksons Reg^t tried, " first, for repeated disobedience of orders — 2^d for abusive language to Major Hull, and refusing to leave his hutt when ordered," unanimously found guilty of the charges exhibited against him, and sentenced to be discharged the service —

The Commander in Chief approves the sentence and orders it to take place. —

BRIGADE ORDERS

Officers of the Day — Capt Lt Symonds
Col^o Crane gives the Orderly to H^d Q^{rs}. —
& Col^o Lamb to the Brigade —

DETAIL FOR GUARDS.

	S	S	C	F & D	M	TOTAL
Crane	—	1	1	—	10	12
Lamb	—	—	1	—	4	5
Procter	—	1	—	—	11	12
Harrison	1	—	—	2	20	23
	1	2	2	2	45	52

10th. June

Officers for Duty   Brig Genl. Poor
     Tomorrow   Lt Col^o Harmer — Major Gaskin
           Brigade Major Mrshall [sic]
        Inspector from Scotts Brigade

Field Officers for Detatchment L'. Coll: Heath
— Major Elison —
For Fatigue, Coll. Brewer, L' Co^{ll} Miller — Major
Hopkinson —

B. Orders

Officers for Day [sic]
    tomorrow   Cap' Singleton
Col° Crane gives the orderly to H Quarters
    Col° Harrison to ye Brigade

Detail

	S	S	C	F	D	M	TOTAL
Crane	1	0	1	1	1	9	13
Lamb	—	1	0	"	"	8	9
Procter	—	—	1	"	"	8	9
Harrison	—	1	"	"	"	20	21
Total	1	2	2	1	1	45	52

— 11th:

Officers
for duty
Tomorrow
{ Major Gen'. Lee —
Brig. Gen¹ Scott —
L' Col° Brent — Major Tubs
Inspector from Penn² Brigade
Brigade Major Minnis.

Some misunderstanding, and mistake in consequence, having arisen with respect to the Major
Generals commands. The Commander in Chief
directs that till a more perfect arrangement can be
made under the new establishment, or till further orders on this head, each Major General is to
command the Division heretofore assigned him,

previous to the late disposition for a march; but in case of an alarm, or any other General Movement of the Army, the three oldest Major Generals present and fit for duty are during the occassion to command the right and left wings and second line of the Army, agreeable to the General Order of the 23ᵈ of May last. The North Carolina Brigade is to supply the place of Maxwells in Lord Stirlings Division, till further orders.

Upon firing the signal guns for an alarm, the Troops are to form immediately in front of their respective Brigades, and are to be marched by the senior Major Generals as above, to their respective alarm posts. ·

The 1ᵗ & 2ᵈ Maryland, and Varnum's Brigades are to draw up in front of their respective encampments and send to the Commander in Chief for orders.

A Major General is to be appointed for the day, who, with the Brigadier and Field Officers on that duty are carefully to attend to the police and good order of the camp. They are always to be on the grand parade at Guard Mounting, and when the Guards are marched off the Major General will make a distribution of the several duties of the day among the Field Officers of it. He is to receive and report to the Commander in Chief all the remarkable occurences which happened during his tour of duty, and will attend in an especial manner to the order of the 9ᵗʰ instant respecting prisoners, as there is reason to believe that many of them are improperly detained in the provost.

All unnecessary waste of Timber is to be avoided.

The Commanding Officers will know that their Q^r Masters attend particularly to this business.

The Commander in Chief having received ample testimony of the general good character and behavior of Lieut Jones, who was sentenced to be dismissed the service by a Genl Court Martial, which sentence was approved by him on the 6th instant; and being further satisfied by Gen^{ls}. Woodford, Scott and other Officers that that Gentleman is not addicted to the vice of gaming, restores him to his rank and command in the Regiment he belonged to, and in the line of the Army.

At a Brigade General Court Martial June 2^d 1778, L^t. Col^o Adams President, Capt. Norwood tried for "refusing to comply with a general order issued expressly for the relief of the Troops on pieket, founded on the necessity of the case, which at that period could not be otherwise remedied," found guilty of the charge exhibited against him and sentenced to be privately reprimanded by the Officer commanding the Reg^t. to which he belongs —

The Commander in Chief utterly disapproves the sentence, as altogether inadequate to the Offence. The mutinous and dangerous spirit which actuated Captain Norwood merited, in his opinion, the most exemplary punishment — He is to be released from his arrest. —

At a Genl Court Martial the 5 Ins^t. Col^o Chambers President, Lt Col^o Hubley of the 10 Penn^a Reg^t. tried for malicious behavior in being the occasion of Col^o Nagle's signing a false return, to the injury of his honor and contrary to good order and military discipline in the case of Capt Long, who as

Col° Hubley told Col° Nagle was absent without leave, tho' he had Col° Hubleys and Gen¹. Waynes orders to remain at Lancaster till the business he was sent on was perfected." After mature deliberation the Court are unanimously of opinion that L⁺ Col° Hubley is not guilty, and do acquit him with honor. — The Commander in Chief confirms the opinion.

At the same Court Cap⁺ Redman of Late Col° Patten's Reg⁺. tried for "misconduct on the night of the 11ᵗʰ of last April; first, in neglecting to guard the passes by which means Cap⁺. Humphry was surprized, — 2ᵈˡʸ not coming to Capt Humphry's assistance when he was attacked by the Enemy " — The Court are unanimously of opinion that Cap⁺. Redman is not guilty of the first charge exhibited against him and do acquit him ; they are of opinion that Capt⁺. Redman is guilty of the 2ᵈ charge but think that his reasons for not marching to the assistance of Cap⁺ Humphry are sufficient and do unanimously acquit him with honor. — The Commander in Chief confirms the opinion of the Court.

At the same Court Willᵐ. Powell, soldier in Col° Angel's Regiment, was tried, " first for desertion, 2ᵈˡʸ for reinlisting — 3ᵈˡʸ. for perjury "—found guilty and sentenced to receive 300 lashes 100 for each crime, and return to Col° Angell's Reg⁺. — The Comʳ. in Chief approves the sentence so far as it extends to 100 lashes —

Likewise Edward Conolly, soldier in Col° Harrison's Reg⁺. of Artillery tried " first for deserting to the enemy — 2ᵈˡʸ. reinlisting into Col° Weltner's Reg⁺." found guilty of the charges exhibited against him and sentenced to receive 200 lashes, 100 for each crime — The Commander in Chief approves the sentence the same as Powell's — These sentences to be put in execution tomorrow morning at the head of the Reg' to which they belong —

The grand parade is assigned in front of Late Conways Brigade.

BRIGADE ORDERS

Officer of the Day, Cap'. Wilkenson
Col° Crane gives the Orderly to Head Q'ˢ.
& Col° Lamb to the Brigade —

DETAIL

	S	S	C	F&D	M	TOTAL
Crane	–	–	–	–	9	9
Lamb	–	–	–	–	8	8
Procter	1	1	–	2	8	12
Harrison	–	1	2	–	20	23
	1	2	2	2	45	52

INDEX

———◆———

51

INDEX

Learned, ——, Brigade Major, 1, 12, 26, 38.

Lee, ——, Captain, 24.

Lee, ——, Major Gen., 9, 14, 16, 35, 43, 46.

Lewis, Thomas, Lieutenant, 15th Virginia Regt., 6.

Lincoln, ——, 14.

Livingston, ——, Lt. Col., 23, 41.

Long, ——, Captain, 48.

McClure, ——, Lt. Col., 2.

McClure, James, Capt. Lt., 2d Continental Artillery, 15.

McCormick, ——, Brigade Major, 5, 32.

McDonald, ——, Lieutenant, 37.

McIntosh's Brigade, 11.

Marks, Isaiah, Lieutenant, 11th Virginia Regt., 7.

Marshall, Elihu, Brigade Major of Poor's Brigade, 20, 45.

Marvin, ——, Brigade Major, 1, 23.

Mauduit du Plessis, Thomas Antoine Chévalier de, 30, 36.

Maxwell, William, Brig. Gen., 4, 47.

Medaras, ——, Captain, 18.

Mentges, Francis, Major, 11th Pennsylvania Regt., 41.

Mercer, John, Captain, 43.

Meredith, ——, Capt. Lt., 43.

Mifflin, Thomas, Major Gen., 14, 35, 37.

Miller, ——, Lt. Col., 23, 46.

Minnis, ——, Brigade Major, 2, 26, 46.

Moore, ——, Major, 5, 39.

Mühlenburg, Peter, Brig. Gen., 5, 11, 23, 26, 33, 38, 43.

Murray, ——, 14.

Nagle, George, Colonel, 10th Pennsylvania Regt., 39, 48, 49.

Nash, Michael, 25.

Nevil, John, 25.

Nixon, ——, Colonel, 7.

North, Caleb, Lt. Col., 11th Pennsylvania Regt., 33.

Norwood, Edward, Captain, 4th Maryland Regt., 48.

Oswald, Eleazer, Lt. Col., 2d Continental Artillery, 15, 25, 26.

Parker, ——, Colonel, 17.

Parks, ——, Lt. Col., 17, 42.

Patten, ——, Major, 10.

Patten, ——, Colonel, 36, 37, 49.

Patterson, Samuel, Brig. Gen., 1, 2, 8, 20, 31, 38, 39.

Pawling, Albert, Major, Malcolm's Additional Continental Regt., 44.

Peters, Andrew, Major, 2d Massachusetts Regt., 36.

Pollard, ——, Major, 3.

Poor, Enoch, Brig. Gen., 4, 12, 20, 31, 38, 45.

Porter, Andrew, Captain, 2d Continental Artillery, 2, 8.

Porter, John, Major, 13th Massachusetts Regt., 32.

Powell, William, Lieutenant, 8, 49, 50.

Powers, William, Capt. Lt., 2d Continental Artillery, 13, 30, 38.

Procter, Thomas, Colonel, 4th Continental Artillery, 4, 5, 7-12, 14, 15, 17, 19, 22, 23, 25, 30, 32, 33, 36, 38, 40, 43, 45, 46, 50.

Ramsey, Nathaniel, Lt. Col., 3d Maryland Regt., 43.

Raymond, Samuel, 3.

Read, Isaac, Colonel, 4th Virginia Regt., 5, 14.

Redman, ——, Captain, 49.

Regnier, ——, Lt. Col., 16, 21, 32.

Reynolds, John, 3.

Rice, Joseph, Captain, 4th Continental Artillery, 38.

Roberts, John, Lieutenant, Malcolm's Additional Continental Regt., 40.

Sargent, Winthrop, Captain, 3d Continental Artillery, 30.

Scott, Charles, Brig. Gen., 4, 7, 14, 16, 33, 38, 45, 46, 48.

Seely, Isaac, Brigade Major, 2d Pennsylvania Brigade, 17.

Selin, Anthony, Captain, 13.

Seward, Thomas, Captain, 3d Continental Artillery, 22.

Shanks, Thomas, 32.

Singleton, Anthony, Captain, 1st Continental Artillery, 46.

Smith, ——, Lt. Col., 41, 44.

Stagg, John, Brigade Major, Conway's Brigade, 8, 36.

Publications of

Lamson, Wolffe & Company

Historical Novels,

In their Relative Chronological Order.

" King Noanett : a Story of Old Virginia and the Massachusetts Bay." By F. J. Stimson (J. S. of Dale). With 12 full-page illustrations by Henry Sandham, R.C.A. $2.00

" Vivian of Virginia : Being the Memoirs of our First Rebellion, by John Vivian, Esq., of Middle Plantation, Virginia." By Hulbert Fuller. With 10 full-page illustrations by Frank T. Merrill. (In press.) $1.75

" The Forge in the Forest : Being the Narrative of the Acadian Ranger, Jean de Mer, Seigneur de Briart, and how he crossed the Black Abbé; and of his Adventures in a Strange Fellowship." By Charles G. D. Roberts. With 7 full-page illustrations by Henry Sandham, R.C.A. $1.50

" A Son of the Old Dominion." By Mrs. Burton Harrison $1.50

" Mademoiselle de Berny : A Story of Valley Forge." By Pauline Bradford Mackie. (In press.) . $1.50

"A Bad Penny." By John T. Wheelwright. With 10 full-page illustrations by F. G. Attwood   . $1.25

"The Pomp of the Lavilettes." By Gilbert Parker $1.25

"A Hero in Homespun: A Tale of the Loyal South." By William E. Barton. With 10 full-page illustrations by Dan Beard $1.50

Other Fiction.

"Don Luis' Wife: A Romance of the West Indies." From her letters and the manuscripts of the Padre, the Doctor Caccavelli, Marc Aurèle, Curate of Samaná. By Lillian Hinman Shuey $1.50

"Miss Träumerei: A Weimar Idyl." By Albert Morris Bagby $1.50

"Zuleka: Being the History of an Adventure in the Life of an American Gentleman, with Some Account of the Recent Disturbances in Dorola." By Clinton Ross $1.50

"At the Queen's Mercy: A Tale of Adventure." By Mabel Fuller Blodgett. With 5 full-page illustrations by Henry Sandham, R.C.A. . . $1.25

"Wives in Exile." A Comedy in Romance, by William Sharp $1.25

"The Gold Fish of Gran Chimú." By Charles F. Lummis. Illustrated by Henry Sandham, R.C.A., with head-pieces drawn by Willard Emery and Arthur T. Clark, and end-pieces by Miss Gwendoline Sandham $1.50

Histories.

" A History of Canada." With Chronological Chart, and
Map of the Dominion of Canada and Newfoundland.
By Charles G. D. Roberts   .   . $2.00, *net*

" Pictures of Russian History and Russian Literature."
(Lowell Lectures.) By Prince Serge Wolkonsky.
With portrait of the author   .   . $2.00, *net*

Poetry.

" Ballads of Lost Haven : A Book of the Sea." By Bliss
Carman .   .   .   .   .   . $1.00, *net*

" Behind the Arras : A Book of the Unseen." By Bliss
Carman. With designs by T. B. Meteyard $1.50, *net*

" Low Tide on Grand Pré : A Book of Lyrics." By
Bliss Carman .   .   .   . $1.00, *net*

" An Opal." By Ednah Proctor Clarke   . $1.00, *net*

" The Book of the Native." By Charles G. D. Roberts
$1.00, *net*

" James Clarence Mangan : His Selected Poems." With
a study by the editor, Louise Imogen Guiney $1.50

" The House of the Trees, and Other Poems." By
Ethelwyn Wetherald.   .   .   . $1.00, *net*

" Skenandoa." By Clinton Scollard .   .   . $1.00

" Giovio and Giulia : A Metrical Romance." By Clinton
Scollard $1.00

"The Viol of Love." By Charles Newton Robinson
$1.50, *net*

"The Love Story of Ursula Wolcott." By Charles
Knowles Bolton. With illustrations by Ethel Reed
$1.00

"The White Wampum: A Book of Indian Verse." By
E. Pauline Johnson   .   .   .   . $1.50, *net*

Juvenile.

"Fairy Tales." By Mabel Fuller Blodgett. With 12
full-page illustrations by Ethel Reed .   . $1.50

"The True Mother Goose." Illustrated and edited by
Blanche McManus. With a historical preface $1.50

Translations.

"The Great Galeoto, and Folly or Saintliness." By José
Echegeray. Translated by Hannah Lynch $1.50, *net*

"Trilby, the Fairy of Argyle." By Charles Nodier.
Translated by Minna Caroline Smith   .   .50

"Magda." A play in four acts. By Hermann Suder-
mann. Translated by Charles-Edward Amory Winslow $1.00

"Vera Vorontzoff." By Sonya Kovalevsky. Translated
by Baroness Anna von Rydingsvärd   .   . $1.25

Short Stories.

"The Merry Maid of Arcady, His Lordship, and Other
Stories." By Mrs. Burton Harrison. Illustrated $1.50

"A Virginia Cousin, and Bar Harbor Tales." By Mrs. Burton Harrison $1.25

"Earth's Enigmas." By Charles G. D. Roberts . $1.25

Miscellaneous.

"Diomed: The Life, Travels, and Observations of a Dog." By John Sergeant Wise. With 100 illustrations by J. Linton Chapman   .   . $2.00

"Ex Libris. Essays of a Collector." By Charles Dexter Allen   .   .   .   .   .   . $3.00, *net*

"Uncle Sam's Church: His Creed, Bible, and Hymn-Book." By John Bell Bouton 50

"Two Unpublished Essays by Ralph Waldo Emerson." With an introduction by Edward Everett Hale $1.00

"'96 Charades." By Norman D. Gray   .   . $1.00

"If Jesus Came to Boston." By Edward Everett Hale .50

"My Double and How He Undid Me." By Edward Everett Hale 75

"Is Polite Society Polite ? and Other Essays." By Mrs. Julia Ward Howe $1.50

"In Friendship's Name."   } Two gift books compiled by
"What Makes a Friend ? "   } Volney Streamer $1.25 each

"Threads of Life." By Clara Sherwood Rollins $1.00

"Orderly Book of General George Washington, Commander in Chief of the American Armies, kept at Valley Forge, 18 May–11 June, 1778 " $1.00, *net*

www.ingramcontent.com/pod-product-compliance
Lightning Source LLC
Chambersburg PA
CBHW021529090426
42739CB00007B/847